Ottawa Hotel

The Ottawa Hotel traveller's guide for Lewiston, Niagara River, Toronto, Lake Ontario and River St. Lawrence

Ottawa Hotel

The Ottawa Hotel traveller's guide for Lewiston, Niagara River, Toronto, Lake Ontario and River St. Lawrence

ISBN/EAN: 9783337211103

Printed in Europe, USA, Canada, Australia, Japan

Cover: Foto ©Andreas Hilbeck / pixelio.de

More available books at **www.hansebooks.com**

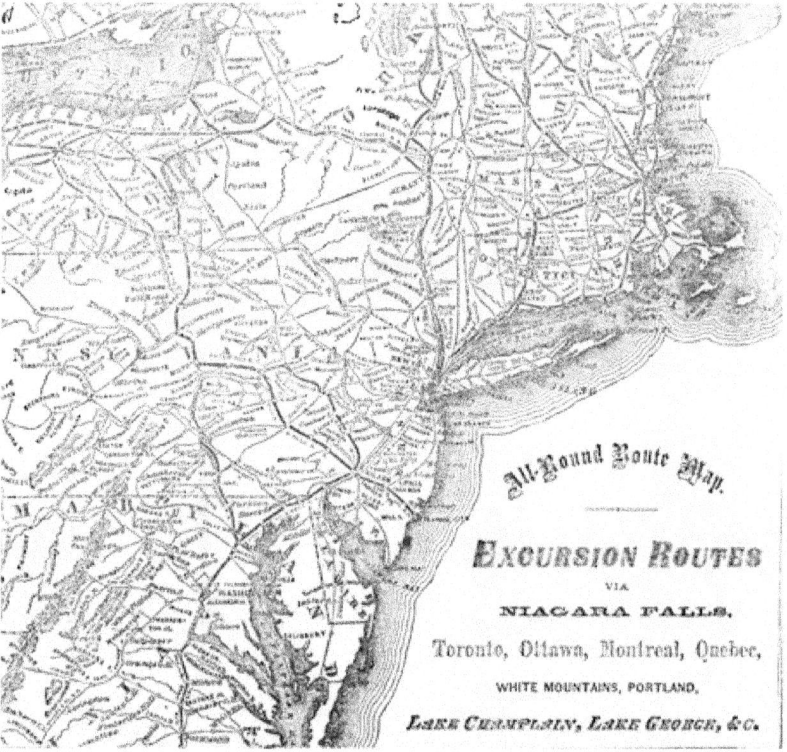

All-Round Route Map.

EXCURSION ROUTES

VIA

NIAGARA FALLS.

Toronto, Ottawa, Montreal, Quebec,

WHITE MOUNTAINS, PORTLAND,

LAKE CHAMPLAIN, LAKE GEORGE, &c.

Hacks & Barouches

CAN BE HAD

By applying at the Office of this House.

~~~~~~~~~~~~~~~~

FOR

Drive Around the Mountain

AND

PRINCIPAL PARTS OF THE CITY,

$4.00.

~~~~~~~~~~~~~~~~

TO LACHINE

AND

Home by the Rapids,

$5.00.

PREFACE.

The Manager of the Ottawa Hotel takes pleasure in presenting to the Tourist his "Guide Book" this season, in an improved dress and enlarged form, and in order to please the Traveller, by the world-renowned trip down the St. Lawrence and its Rapids, has added additional matter, giving a more full description of the various places on the Route, and a more particular description of each Rapid; he has spared neither labour nor expense to make this a thoroughly reliable book, and it is presented by his Agent, "gratis," to the Traveller, thereby affording as good, if not better, information than is found in a "Route Guide," for which the Tourist is charged fifty cents or one dollar. No other Guide now before the public is either sufficiently recent or comprehensive to be safely followed by the Tourist from Niagara Falls to the far-famed Saguenay River. It is not without confidence, therefore, that I commit this Hand-Book as a reliable and much needed one, to the Travelling Public.

Very respectfully,

C. S. BROWNE,
Manager.

LEWISTON.

This village is situated at the head of navigation, on the Lower Niagara, and is a place of considerable importance. It lies three miles below the Devil's Hole, and seven miles below the Falls. Lewiston is a pleasant, well built village, but its commercial prospects have been very much injured by the construction of the Erie and Welland Canals.

QUEENSTON.

Is a small village, situated nearly opposite to Lewiston, and contains about 200 inhabitants. It is the Canadian termination of the Bridge, and is associated in history with the gallant defence made by the British on the adjacent heights in the war of 1812. The village is pleasantly situated, but it has suffered from the same causes that have retarded the growth of Lewiston. Near this point the river becomes more tranquil, the shores appear less broken and wild, and the change in the scenery affords a pleasing transition from the sublime to the beautiful.

BROCK'S MONUMENT.

The Monument stands on the Heights of Queenston from whence the village derives its name. The present structure occupies the site of the former one, which was blown up by some miscreant, on the 17th of April, 1840. The whole edifice is four hundred and eighty-five feet high; on the sub-base, which is forty feet square and thirty feet high, are placed four lions, facing north, south, east, and west; the base of the pedestal is twenty-one and a half feet square, and ten feet high; the pedestal itself is sixteen feet square, and ten feet high, surmounted with a heavy cornice, ornamented with lion's heads and wreaths, in alto-relievo. In ascending from the top of the pedestal to the top of the base of the shaft, the form changes from square to round. The shaft is a fluted column of freestone, seventy-five feet high and ten feet in diameter; on which stands a Corinthian capital, ten feet high, whereon is wrought, in relief, a statue of the Goddess of War. On this capital is the dome, nine feet high, which is reached by 250 spiral steps from the base, on the inside. On the top of the dome is placed a colossal statue of Gen. Brock.

FORT NIAGARA.

This Fort stands at the mouth of the Niagara River on the American side. There are many interesting associations connected with the spot; as, during the earlier part of the past century, it was the scene of many severe conflicts between the Whites and the Indians, and subsequently between the English and the French. The names of the heroic La Salle, the courtly De Nouville, and the gallant Prideaux, will

long retain a place in the history of this country.
The village adjacent to the Fort is called Youngs-
town, in honour of its founder, the late John Young,
Esq.

NIAGARA

Is one of the oldest towns in Upper Canada, and was
formerly the capital of the Province. It is situated
where the old town of Newark stood, and is opposite
to Youngstown. It faces the river on one side, and
Lake Ontario on the other. The trade of this place
has been diverted to St. Catherines since the completion of the Welland Canal; and the other towns
upon the Niagara River have suffered in common,
from the same cause.

TORONTO

the Capital City in Upper Canada, is situated on an
arm of Lake Ontario, thirty-six miles from the mouth
of Niagara River. This city was formerly called
Little York. The first survey was made in 1793.
Toronto Bay is a beautiful inlet, seperated from the
main body of Lake Ontario, except at its entrance,
by a long, narrow, sandy beach. The south-western
extremity is called Gibraltar Point. The population,
in 1817, was 1200; but at the present time it amounts
to about 60,000. With a similar progress for a few
years to come, the population of this city will be
second to none in British America. Among the principal buildings of Toronto, are a University and a
Cathedral. One of the ecclesiastical edifices deserves
especial notice,—the Church of the Holy Trinity; a
handsome structure, erected by a donation of five
thousand pounds from some liberal person from
England, on condition that the whole of the seats

should be free The Elgin Association, for improving
the moral and religious condition of the colored
population, is among the most useful institutions of
the place. That stupendous undertaking, the Grand
Trunk Railway of Canada, passes through Toronto,
and promises a splendid future, not only for this city
but for every other city in the country ; for the benefits
to be derived from it are incalculable. Nature has
bestowed fine rivers and vast lakes, which have already
been made fully subservient to commerce; but how
wonderfully will commerce be advanced by the linking
of these lakes and rivers by means of railways. Thus
will be constituted one great unbroken medium of
speedy communication from the far West of America
to the shores of the Atlantic.

PORT HOPE

is situated sixty-five miles from Toronto. A small
stream, which here falls into the Lake, has formed a
valley, in which the town is located. The harbor
formed at the mouth of this stream is shallow, but
safe and commodious. Port Hope is a very pretty
town ; on the western side the hills rise gradually one
above another. The highest summit, which is called
" Fort Orton," affords a fine prospect, and overlooks
the country for a great distance around. The village
is incorporated, and contains about 2,200 inhabitants.

COBOURG

lies seven miles below Port Hope, and contains 4000
inhabitants. The town contains seven churches, two
banks, three grist mills, two foundries, and the largest
cloth factory in the province. It is also the seat of

Victoria College and a Theological Institute. Midway between Port Hope and Cobourg, is " Duck Island," on which a lighthouse is maintained by the government.

KINGSTON.

This place was called by the Indians "*Cataracqui.*" A settlement was begun by the French, under De Courcelles, as early as 1672. The Fort which was finished the next year, was called Fort Frontenac, in honor of the French Count of that name. This Fort was alternately in the possession of the French and the Indians, until it was destroyed by the expedition under Col. Bradstreet, in 1758. In 1762, the place fell into the hands of the English, from whom it received its present name. Kingston was one of the most important military posts in Canada. It is one hundred and ten miles from Cobourg, and contains about 11,000 inhabitants.

[Before proceeding down the St. Lawrence, we will retrace our steps, and briefly notice the places on the American side of Lake Ontario.]

OSWEGO

is the next port after passing Charlottesville. It is a beautiful and flourishing town, and contains a population of about 15,000. It is the commercial centre of a fertile and wealthy part of the country, and is the terminus of a railroad and a canal, connecting it with Syracuse and the New York Central Railway. The history of this place is associated with many hard battles, fought during the time of the Indian and French wars.

SACKETT'S HARBOUR

Is situated about forty-five miles from Oswego, and twenty miles from the St. Lawrence. It lies upon the north-eastern shore of Lake Ontario, and derives its name from Mr. Sackett, of Jamacia, L. I., who purchased and took possession of it in 1799. It is admirably fitted, from its position, for a naval station, and is now the seat of a military post, called "Madison Barracks."

THE THOUSAND ISLANDS

are amongst the wonders of the St. Lawrence, situated about six miles below Kingston. There are in fact no less than 1,800 of these "emerald gems in the ring of the wave," of all sizes, from the islet a few yards square to miles in length. It is a famous spot for sporting ; myriads of wild fowl of all descriptions may here be found ; and angling is rather fatiguing than otherwise, from the great quantity and size of the fish. These Islands too, have been the scene of most exciting romance. From their great number, and the labyrinth-like channels among them, they afforded an admirable retreat for the insurgents in the last Canadian insurrection, and for the American sympathizers with them, who, under the questionable name of "patriots," sought only to embarrass the British Government. Among these was one man, who, from his daring and ability, became an object of anxious pursuit to the Canadian authorities ; and he found a safe asylum in these watery intricacies, through the devotedness and courage of his daughter, whose inimitable management of her canoe was such, that through hosts of pursuers, she baffled their efforts at capture,

while she supplied him with provisions in these solitary retreats, rowing him from one place of conceal-
ment to another, under shadow of the night. But, in
truth all the Islands, which are so numerously stud-
ded through the whole chain of those magnificent
Lakes, abound with materials for romance and poe-
try. For instance, in the Manitoulin Islands, in Lake
Huron, the Indians believe that the *Manitou*, that is,
the *Great Spirit* (and hence the name of the islands)
has forbidden his children to seek for gold ; and they
tell you that a certain point, where it is reported to
exist in large quantities, has never been visited by the
disobedient Indian, without his canoe being over-
whelmed in a tempest.

CLAYTON.

This village is situated on the American side,
opposite the " Thousand Islands," and was formerly
of considerable importance as a lumber station.
Square timber and staves were here made up into
large rafts, and floated down the St. Lawrence to
Montreal and Quebec. These rafts were often very
large; and as they require a great number of men to
navigate them, the huts erected for their shelter give
them, as they pass down the river, the appearance of
small villages. Many of the steamers and other
craft that navigate Lake Ontario were built here, and
during the past five years Clayton has become a great
resort for pleasure seekers; " the fishing and shooting
is the best in the St. Lawrence, the late Geo.
Peabody, Esq., has spent several weeks here each
season when in this country for the last five years, to
enjoy the sports of fishing, shooting, bathing, etc.,
other celebrities could be named also," who make
their annual visits here, the beauty of the Islands and

River at this place cannot be surpassed—there are also two good hotels that are filled with pleasure seekers during the summer months, the Johnston House fronts the River and is near the Steamboat Landing, and the Hubbard House, near the centre of the town, both enjoy good reputations.

ALEXANDRIA BAY

is the next port after leaving Clayton. It is built upon a massive pile of rocks, and its situation is romantic and highly picturesque. It is a place of resort for sportsmen. Some two or three miles below the village, is a position from whence one hundred islands can be seen at one view. This place also is celebrated for its fishing and shooting. The beauty of the Islands in this vicinity for several miles up and down the River can hardly be imagined without a personal visit. There is a great quantity of fish killed here known as the Mascolonge, they are of large size, many of them weighing forty to fifty and often as high as seventy pounds, they are taken with trolling lines and it requires a skilful angler to land one safely. Sportsmen consider the taking of one of these fish equal to Salmon fishing. There is a good Hotel here which is filled with visitors during the Summer. The Crossman House, H. Crossman, Proprietor.

BROCKVILLE

was named in honour of General Brock, who fell on Queenston Heights, in the war of 1812. It is situated on the Canadian side of the St. Lawrence, and is one of the pleasantest villages in the province. It is situated at the foot of the Thousand Islands, on an

elevation of land which rises from the river in a suc-
cession of ridges. The town was laid out in 1802,
and is now a place of considerable importance. The
present population is about 4000. It is growing very
rapidly, and is one of the most pleasant, healthy and
thriving towns on this side of the river.

OGDENSBURG.

In the year 1748, the Abbe François Piquet, who
was afterwards styled the "Apostle of the Iroquois,"
was sent to establish a mission at this place, as many
of the Indians of that tribe had manifested a desire
of embracing Christianity. A settlement was begun
in connection with this mission, and a fort, called
"La Presentation," was built at the mouth of the
Oswegatchie, on the west side. The remains of the
walls of this Fort are still to be seen. In October,
1749, it was attacked by a band of Indians from the
Mohawks, who, although bravely repulsed, succeeded
in destroying the pallisades of the fort and two of the
vessels belonging to the colony. The Abbe Piquet
retired from the settlement soon after the defeat of
Montcalm, and finally returned to France, where he
died in 1781.

In describing the situation of the ground on the
east side of the river, opposite to his fort, the Abbe,
with his accustomed discrimination, remarked: "A
beautiful town could hereafter be built here." This
prediction has been fully verified; and the city of
Ogdensburgh now occupies this site. It has in-
creased rapidly within the past few years, and will
doubtless become a large manufacturing place. The
Northern Railroad, which runs to Lake Champlain,
a distance of one hundred and eighteen miles, and
which connects at Rouse's Point with the railroads to

Boston and Montreal, has its terminus here. We may add that in time it will be a large city, as it continues to grow rapidly, and is one of the wealthiest cities of its size in the State of New-York. The streets are wide, and lined with beautiful shade trees, and the private residences some of them are magnificent, and the public buildings are very fine. It is also a great resort during the summer season for pleasure seekers, and being the terminus of the Ogdensburgh and Rome Railroad, it is one of the principal points for travellers to take the steamers down the Rapids, for Montreal. The principal Hotel at Ogdensburg, is the Seymour House—F. J. Tallman, proprietor.

PRESCOTT

is situated on the Canada side of the St. Lawrence, opposite Ogdensburg, and contains about 3000 inhabitants. Previous to the opening of the Rideau Canal between Kingston and Ottawa City (formerly Bytown) Prescott was a place of importance in the carrying trade between Kingston and Montreal; but since that event its growth has been checked. Matters have, however, again changed, and for Prescott there are prospects of brighter days to come. Through the influence, and energy, and untiring perseverance of Robert Bell, Esq., of Ottawa City, a railroad has been built, under almost insurmountable obstacles, which extends from Ottawa City to Prescott, and there connects the Ottawa River with the St. Lawrence. The enterprise has, thus far, more than realized the most sanguine hopes of its projector. About a mile below the town of Prescott, at a placed called " Windmill Point," are the ruins of an old stone windmill, in which, in 1837, the " Patriots," under Von Shultz, a Polish exile, established themselves, but from which they were driven with severe loss. About five miles below Prescott is Chimney Island, on which the remains of an old French fortification are to be seen. The first rapid of the St. Lawrence is at this Island.

THE GALOP RAPID.

The next town on the American side is Waddington ; and in the river, over against it, is Ogden Island. On the Canada side is Morrisburg, formerly called West Williamsburg. It is called the Port of Morristown, and contains about two hundred inhabitants. A short distance below Morristown, on the Canada side is Chrysler's farm, where in 1813, a battle was fought between the English and the Americans. The Americans were commanded by Gen. Wilkinson, and were at that time descending the **river** to attack Montreal. The attempt was afterwards abandoned. Thirty miles below Ogdensburg, is Louisville, from whence stages run to Massena Springs, distant seven miles.

LONG SAULT.

A continuous rapid of 9 miles, divided in the centre by an island. The usual passage for steamers is on the south side. The channel on the north side was formerly considered unsafe and dangerous ; but examinations have been made, and it is now descended with safety. The passage in the southern channel is very narrow, and such is the velocity of the current that a raft, it is said, will drift the nine miles in forty minutes.

DESCENT OF THE RAPIDS.

This is the most exciting part of the whole passage of the St. Lawrence. The rapids of the " Long Sault " rush along at the rate of something like twenty miles an hour. When the vessel enters within their influence the steam is shut off and she is carried onwards by the force of the stream alone. The surging waters present all the angry appearance of the Ocean in a storm ; the noble boat strains and labors : but unlike the ordinary pitching and tossing at sea, this going down hill by water produces a highly novel sensation, and is, in fact, a service of some danger, the imminence of which is enhanced to the imagination by the tremendous roar of the headlong boiling current. Great nerve, and force, and precision are here required in piloting, so as to keep the vessel's head straight with the course of the rapid ; for if she diverges in the least, presenting her side to the current, or " broached to," as the nautical phrase is, she would be instantly run aground. Hence the necessity of enormous power over her rudder; and for this purpose the mode of steering affords great facility, for the wheel that governs the rudder is placed ahead, and by means of chain and pulley sways it. But in descending the rapids a tiller is placed astern to the rudder itself, so that the tiller can be manned as well as the wheel, Some idea may be entertained of the peril of descending a rapid, when it requires four men at the wheel and two at the tiller to ensure safe steering. Here is the region of the daring raftsmen, at whose hands are demanded infinite courage and skill ; there is however but little danger to life, as it frequently happens that a steamer strikes, and sinks, but a few minutes puts them safely in shoal water. The Canadian Navigation

Company have never lost any lives by accidents of this kind in descending the rapids.

ST. LAWRENCE CANALS.

	Miles.	Locks.	L. Ft.
Galops Canal,.....................	2	2	8.
Point Iroquois Canal......	3	1	6.
Rapid Platt Canal..................	4	2	11.6
Farlen's Point Canal................	¾	1	4.
Cornwall Canal, Long Sault..........	11½	7	48.
Beauharnois Canal, Coteau			
Cedars, Split Rock, Cascade Rapids....	11¼	9	82.6
Lachine Canal, Lachine Rapids........	8½	5	44.9
Fall on portions of the St. Lawrence between canals from Lake Ontario to Montreal......................	......	......	17.
From Montreal to tide water at Three Rivers...............*......	......	......	12.9
	41	27	234.½

The St. Lawrence Canal was designed for paddle-steamers, but from the magnitude of the rapids and their regular inclination the aid of the locks is not required in descending the river. Large steamers, drawing seven feet water, with passengers and the mails, leave the foot of Lake Ontario in the morning, and reach the wharves of Montreal by daylight, without passing through a single lock. At some of the rapids there are obstacles preventing the descent of deeply laden craft; but the government are about to give the main channel in all the rapids a depth of ten feet water, when the whole descending trade by steam will keep the river, leaving the canals to ascending craft.

CORNWALL.

A pleasant town situated at the foot of the Long Sault,

on the Canada side. Here vessels are passed up the river by the Cornwall canal and come out into the river about twelve miles above. The boundary line between the United States and Canada passes near this village, and the course of the St. Lawrence is hereafter within Her Majesty's dominions.

ST. REGIS

is an old Indian village, and lies a little below Cornwall, on the opposite side of the river. It contains a Catholic church, which was built about the year 1700. While the building was in progress, the Indians were told by their priest that a bell was indispensable in their house of worship, and they were ordered to collect furs sufficient to purchase one. The furs were collected, the money was sent to France, and the bell was bought and shipped for Canada; but the vessel which contained it was captured by an English cruiser, and taken into Salem, Massachusetts. The bell was afterwards purchased for the Church at Deerfield. The priest of St. Regis, having heard of its destination, excited the Indians to a general crusade for its recovery. They joined the expedition fitted out by the Governor against the New England colonists, and proceeded through the then long, trackless wilderness, to Deerfield, which they attacked in the night. The inhabitants, unsuspicious of danger, were aroused from sleep only to meet the tomahawk and scalping knife of the savages. Forty-seven were killed, and one hundred and twelve taken captive; among whom were Mr. Williams, the pastor and his family. Mrs. Williams being at the time feeble, and not able to travel with her husband and family, was killed by the Indians. Mr. Williams and a part of his surviving family afterwards returned to Deerfield, but the others remained with the Indians, and became connected with the tribe. The Rev. Eleazar Williams, one of the supposed descendants from this family, has been mysteriously identified with the lost Dauphin of France. The Indians after having completed their work of destruction, fastened the bell to a long pole, and carried it upon their shoulders a distance of nearly one hundred and fifty miles, to the place where Burlington now stands , they buried it there, and in the following spring removed it to the church of St. Regis where it now hangs.

LAKE ST. FRANCIS.

This is the name of that expansion of the St. Lawrence which begins near Cornwall, and St. Regis, and extends to Coteau du Lac, a distance of forty miles. The surface of this lake is interpersed with a great number of small islands. The village of Lancaster is situated on the northern side, about midway of this lake.

COTEAU DU LAC

is a small village, situated at the foot of Lake St. Francis. The name as well as the style of the buildings, denotes its French origin. Just below the village are the Coteau Rapids.

At Coteau du Lac, fifty miles (by water) above Montreal, commences a rapid of the same extent, extending about two miles.

Seven miles below this commences the Cedar Rapid, which extends about three miles, then comes the Coteau Cedar, Split Rock and Cascade Rapids, which terminate at the head of Lake St. Louis, where the dark waters of the Ottawa, by one of its mouths, join the St.

Lawrence. These rapids in eleven miles have a descent of 82½ feet.

CEDARS.

The village presents the same marks of French origin as Coteau du Lac. In the expedition of Gen. Amherst, a detachment of three hundred men, that were sent to attack Montreal, were lost in the rapids near this place. The passage through these rapids is very exciting. There is a peculiar motion of the vessel, which in descending seems like settling down, as she glides from one ledge to another. In passing the rapids of the Split Rock, a person unacquainted with the Navigation of these rapids will almost involuntarily hold his breath until this ledge of rocks, which is distinctly seen from the deck of the steamer, is passed. At one time the vessel seems to be running directly upon it, and you feel certain that she will strike; but a skillful hand is at the helm, and in an instant more it is passed in safety.

BEAUHARNOIS

is a small village at the foot of the Cascades, on the south bank of the river. Here vessels enter the Beauharnois canal, and pass around the rapids of the Cascades, Cedars and Coteau, into Lake St. Francis, a distance of fourteen miles. On the north bank, a branch of the Ottawa enters into the St. Lawrence. The river again widens into a lake called St. Louis. From this place a view is had of Montreal Mountain, nearly thirty miles distant. In this lake is Nun's Island, which is beautifully cultivated, and belongs to the Grey Nunnery, at Montreal. There are many islands in the vicinity of Montreal belonging to the different nunneries, and from which they derive large revenues.

LACHINE.

This village is nine miles from Montreal, with which it is connected by railroad. The Lachine Rapids, begin just below the town. The current is here so swift and wild that to avoid it a canal has been cut around these rapids. This canal is a stupendous work, and reflects much credit upon the energy and enterprise of the people of Montreal.

CAUGHNAWAGA,

an Indian village lying on the south bank of the river, near the entrance of the Lachine Rapids, derived its name from the Indians that had been converted by the Jesuits, who were called " *Caughnawagas*," or " praying Indians." This was probably a misnomer, for they were distinguished for their predatory incursions upon their neighbors in the New England provinces. The bell that now hangs in their church was the proceeds of one of these excursions. It is at this place the old Indian pilot shoots out in his bark canoe and boards the steamer for the purpose of piloting her down the Lachine Rapids. *Baptiste*, the old Indian pilot, is as anxiously looked for by passengers on board of steamers down the Lachine Rapids as the Rapid itself; he is now an old man being about sixty years of age, and has made it his business for over forty years to pilot steamers down the Rapids and has not missed a day in twenty years; during the summer season he is employed exclusively by the Canadian Navigation Co. The village of Laprairie, is some seven miles below Caughnawaga.

The Lachine Rapids, a few miles above Montreal, are the last rapids of importance that occur on the St. Lawrence, are now considered the most difficult of navigation. They are obviated by the Lachine canal, 8½ miles in length, overcoming a descent of 44½ feet.

And now the traveller comes to the last wonder of the present age, namely the Victoria Bridge, spanning the noble St. Lawrence River, two miles long, the longest and largest bridge in the world, after which the delighted traveller comes in full view of the city of Montreal, the most prominent object being the two towers of the church of Notre Dame.

CITY OF MONTREAL.

The City of Montreal is the largest and most populous city in British North America. It was founded by Mr. de Maisonneuve, in 1642, on the site of an Indian village named Hochelaga, and dedicated to the Virgin Mary as its patroness and its protector, and for a long period bore the name of *Ville Marie*. It is laid in the form of a parallelogram, and contains some two hundred streets, with a population of over 130,000.

The traveller in approaching the city from the river, is struck with the peculiar beauty of the large cut stone buildings which front the majestic river St. Lawrence, on whose banks they are reared, resembling in their solid masonry and elegance the building of European cities.

The Island of Montreal is, in fact, most properly regarded as the garden of Canada. The city being at the head of ship navigation, her local advantages are unsurpassed.

PLACES OF INTEREST.

Among the many substantial and elegant edifices in the city of recent completion, may be mentioned—

The New Court House, on Notre Dame street, and directly opposite to Nelson's Monument, is of elegant cut stone in the Grecian Ionic style. The ground plan is 300 by 125 ft. ; height 76 feet.

The Post Office, on Great St. James Street, is a beautiful cut stone building.

The Merchants' Exchange, situated on St. Sacrament street.

The Mechanics' Institute, a very fine building situated on Great St. James street, of cut stone, three storeys high, built in the Italian style. The lecture Room is tastefully decorated.

The Mercantile Library Association Building, Bonaventure Street.

The Bank of Montreal, Place d'Armes, St. James Street, opposite the Cathedral, an elegant cut stone building of the Corinthian order.

The City Bank, next to the above, in the Grecian style of cut stone, and worthy of note.

The Bank of British North America, Great St. James street, next to the Post Office, is a handsome building of cut stone, and built in the composite style of architecture.

Molson's Bank, Great St. James street, is a handsome structure, built of Ohio sandstone. *The finest* in the City.

The Bonsecours Market, on St. Paul and Water streets, is a magnificent edifice in the Grecian and Doric style ; cost about $300,000 ; has a front of three storys on Water street, and two storys on St. Paul. The upper part of the building is occupied by the various officers of the city. The City Council Room is fitted up in the most elegant style. In the east wing of the building is a large hall or concert room.

The McGill College.—This is an institution of very high repute. It was founded by the Hon. James McGill, who bequeathed a valuable estate and £10,000 for its endowment. The buildings for the Faculty of Arts are delightfully situated at the base of the mountain, and command an extensive view.

The wharves of the city are unsurpassed by any on the American Continent. They are built of wood and meeting with the locks and cut stone wharves of Lachine, they present for several miles a display of continuous wharfage which has few parallels. Unlike the levees of the Ohio and Mississipi, no unsightly warehouses disfigure the river side. A broad terrace, faced with grey limestone, the parapets of which are surmounted with a substantial iron railing, divides the City from the river throughout its whole extent.

The remaining public buildings worthy of notice are : the Old Government House, Notre Dame street, now occupied as the Normal School ; the Barracks ; the Custom House, St. Paul street, the Bon Pasteur Nunnery ; Hotel-Dieu Hospital, Sherbrooke street ; Church of the Gesu, Bleury street.

Mount Royal Cemetery is situated on the east side of the mountain, about two miles from the city. Judgment and taste have been displayed in the selec- tion and management of the grounds ; it is much visited by strangers.

The Champ de Mars.—This is a favorite promenade for citizens and strangers, being the general parade and review ground of the military, and is frequently enlivened during the summer evenings by music from the fine bands of the regiments.

Viger Square, near the Champ de Mars, is beautifully laid out into a garden, with conservatory, fountains, &s. Place d'Armes is a handsome square between Notre Dame and St. James streets, opposite the French Cathedral. It is surrounded by a neat iron railing, and tastefully laid out and planted with shade trees; in the centre of the square is a fountain.

The Victoria Bridge—The cost of this gigantic structure was originally estimated at £1,450,000, but this sum has since been reduced and the present calculation of its cost is about £1,250,000. In it 250,000 tons of stone, and 7,500 tons of iron have been used. The iron superstructure is supported by 24 piers and two abutments. The centre span is 330 feet; there are 12 spans each side of the centre of 242 feet each. The extreme length, including abutments, is 7,000 feet. The height above summer water level in the centre opening is 60 feet, descending to either end at the rate of 1 in 130. The contents of the masonry is 3,000,000 of cubic feet. The weight of iron in the tubes is 8,000 tons. The following are the dimensions of the tubes through which the trains pass in the middle span, viz,: 22 feet high, 16 feet wide, at the extreme ends, 19 feet high and 16 wide.

The total length from the river bank, is 10,284 feet, or about 50 yards less than two English miles.

The Lachine Canal is among the public works particularly worthy of note, and of which the city may well feel proud. The head of water on this canal has been rendered available for the creation of water power, which has been applied most successfully to the movements of very extensive machinery over a large extent of ground. Among the works here are founders, engine and boiler shops, ship yard and marine works, saw mills, sash, blind, and door factories, flour mills, cotton mills, edge tool factories, &c., &c.

As a place of beauty and pleasure, the ride from the city around Mount Royal will attract the traveller at all times. The distance is nine miles, commanding one of the finest views of beautiful landscape to be found in North America, and in returning, entering the city a view of the St. Lawrence and of Montreal, both comprehensive and extended, that well repays time and expense.

Next to the drive around the mountain is that on the Lachine road, leading to a village of that name, nine miles from the city. The road is directly along the banks of the river presenting scenery of unsurpassed beauty and grandeur. It is a lovely drive. If the proper hour is selected, a view may be had of the descent of the steamer over the rapids.

Another favorite drive in the immediate vicinity is to Longue Pointe, being in an opposite direction from the last, and down along the banks of the river.

It would be useless to undertake an enumeration of all the places of interest in and about Montreal, for we believe that there are but few places on the American Continent where can be found so much of interest to the traveller, whether in pursuit of health or pleasure, as in this city.

RAILROAD AND STEAMBOAT OFFICES.—Grand Trunk Railway Offices, for Quebec, Portland, Toronto, at Bonaventure Station.

Depot—Bonaventure street.

Upper Canada Line of Steamers—177 Great St. James street.

Ottawa City Steamboat Office—Mercantile Library Building, Bonaventure street. Passengers go via Lachine Railroad, Bonaventure Depot.

Quebec Steamboat Office—29 Commissioners street.

☞ All stages and omnibuses to and from the cars and steamers call at the Ottawa Hotel.

☞ Parties of pleasure or on business, who desire carriages, will be accommodated by leaving their orders at the office.

CURRENCY.—Canada pound, $4; Canada Shillings, 20 cents;

Canada Sixpence, **10** cents; British Sixpence, 12 cents; British Shilling, 24 cents.

FARE PER HOUR.—Coaches, or four-wheeled cabs, or corresponding winter vehicles, drawn by two horses, for the first hour $1. For each subsequent hour 75 cents, and *pro rata* for intermediate quarters of an hour.

Cabs, two or four-wheeled, or corresponding winter vehicles, drawn by one horse, for one or two persons, for the first hour 50 cents, and for each subsequent hour 40 cents. For three or four persons, for the first hour 75 cents; each subsequent hour 50 cents, and *pro rata* for intermediate quarters of an hour.

Usual charges for two-horse carriages to go round the **mountain**, a distance of nine miles, $4. for one or four persons.

For cab, $1.50 for two or three persons; for four persons, $2.

LAKE ST. PETER

is an expansion of the St. Lawrence, beginning about five miles below Sorel, and extending in length twenty-five miles; its greatest breadth being nine miles. There are several islands at its western extremity. Port St. Francis is a small village, situated on the south shore of Lake **St.** Peter, eighty-two miles below Montreal. It is a place of but little importance.

THREE RIVERS

is situated at the confluence of the rivers St. Maurice and St. Lawrence, ninety miles below Montreal, and the same distance above Quebec. It is one of the oldest settled towns in Canada, having been founded in 1618. It is well laid out, and contains many good buildings, among which are the Court House, the goal, the Roman Catholic Church, the Ursuline Convent, and the English and Wesleyan churches. The population of Three Rivers is about 5,500.

BASTICAN

is situated on the north shore of the river, one hundred and seventeen miles below Montreal. It is the last place at which the steamers stop before reaching Quebec. It is a place of little importance.

In passing down the St. Lawrence from Montreal, the country upon its banks presents a sameness in its general scenery, until we approach the vicinity of Quebec. The villages and hamlets are decidedly *French* in character, and are generally made up of small buildings, the better class of which are painted white or white-washed, with red roofs. Prominent in the distance appear the tile-covered spires of the Catholic churches, which are all constructed in that unique style of architecture so peculiar to that church.

The rafts of timber afford a highly interesting feature on the river as the traveller passes along. On each a shed is built for the raftsmen, some of whom rig out their huge, unwieldy craft with gay streamers, which flutter from the tops of poles. Thus, when several of these rafts are grappled together, forming as it were, a floating island of timber, half a mile wide and a mile long, the sight is extremely picturesque; and when the voices of these hardy sons of the forest and the stream join in some of their Canadian boat songs, the wild music, borne by the breeze along the water, has a charming effect. Myriads of these rafts may be seen lying in the coves at Quebec, ready to be shipped to the different parts of the world.

CITY OF QUEBEC.

Quebec, by its historic fame and its unequalled scenery, is no ordinary or commonplace city, for though like other large communities it carries on trade, commerce and manufactures; cultivates arts, science and literature; abounds in charities, and professes special regard to the amenities of social life, it claims particular attention as being a strikingly unique old place, the stronghold of Canada, and, in fact, the key of the Province. Viewed from any one of its approaches, it impresses the stranger with the conviction of strength and permanency. The reader of American history on entering its gates, or wandering over its squares, ramparts and battle fields, puts himself at once in communion with the illustrious dead. The achievements of daring mariners, the labors of self-sacrificing missionaries of the cross, and the conflicts of military heroes, who bled and died in the assault and defence of its walls, are here re-read with ten-fold interest. Then the lover of nature in her grandest and most rugged, as in her gentle and most smiling forms, will find in and around it, an affluence of sublime and beautiful objects. The man of science, too, may be equally gratified, for here the great forces of nature and her secret alchemy may be studied with advantage. Quebec can never be a tame or insipid place, and with moderate opportunities for advancement, it must become one of the greatest cities of the new world in respect of learning, arts, commerce and manufactures.

The city of Quebec was founded by Samuel Champlain, 1608. In 1622 the population was reduced to fifty souls.

In June, 1759, the English army under Gen. Wolfe landed upon the Island of Orleans. On the 12th September took place the celebrated battle of the Plains of Abraham, which resulted in the death of Wolfe, and the defeat of the French army. A force of 5,000 English troops under Gen. Murray were left to garrison the fort.

The city is very interesting to a stranger ; it is the only walled city in Canada.

Cape Diamond, upon which the citadel stands, is three hundred and forty-five feet in height, and derives its name from the quantity of crystal mixed with the granite below its surface. The fortress includes the whole space on the Cape.

Above the spot where General Montgomery was killed, is now the inclined plane, running to the top of the bank ; it is five hundred feet long, and is used by the Government to convey stores and other articles of great weight to the fortress. Strangers are allowed to enter this fortress by procuring tickets from the proper authorities.

A ride to the Plains of Abraham is one of the most interesting visits about this celebrated city ; a rock is there pointed out as the spot where General Wolfe expired. There are four martello towers, forty feet in height, standing upon the plain, about half a mile in advance of the other fortifications.

Seven miles below Quebec is the Fall of Montmorency. The road is very pleasant, passing through the French village of Beauport. Those who expect to see a second Niagara will be very much disappointed. The stream descends in silvery threads, over a precipice two hundred and forty feet in height, and, in connection with the surrounding scenery, is extremely picturesque and beautiful, but inspires none of the awe felt at Niagara.

The French Catholic Church is a spacious stone building, and the interior is decorated with some fine paintings. Since the destruction of the convent at Charlestown, Mass., Americans are not allowed entrance to the Ursuline Convent. It is the more to be regretted from the fact that the grave of Montcalm is in their chapel.

Castle St. Louis, probably the first building in Quebec, the corner stone of which was laid by Champlain on the 6th of May, 1624, was destroyed by fire on the 23rd of January, 1834. By the orders of Lord Durham, the site of the castle was cleared of the ruins that covered it, levelled and covered with wood, and an iron railing placed on the edge of the precipice, making a very delightful promenade. The view from it commands the lower town, the St. Lawrence as far down as the Island of Orleans, the harbor with its ships, and Point Levi on the opposite side of the river.

Point Levi, on the other side of the River opposite Quebec, will interest the stranger very much ; immense and stupendous fortifications being now in progress of construction.

RIVER SAGUENAY.

To the pleasure seeker, or to the man of science, there can be nothing more refreshing and delightful, nothing affording more food for reflection or scientific observation, than a trip to that most wonderful of rivers, the Saguenay.

On the way thither, the scenery of the Lower St. Lawrence is extraordinarily picturesque ; a broad expanse of water interpersed with rugged solitary islets, highly cultivated islands, and islands covered with trees to the water's edge, hemmed in by lofty and precipitous mountains on the one side and by a continuous street of houses, relieved by beautifully situated villages, the spires of whose tin covered churches glitter in the sunshine, affords a prospect so enchanting, that were nothing else to be seen, the tourist would be well repaid ; but when in addition to all this the tourist suddenly passes from a landscape unsurpassed for beauty into a region of primitive grandeur, where art has done nothing and nature everything, when at a single bound, civilization is left behind, and nature stares him in the face, in naked majesty; when he sees Alps on Alps arise ; when he floats over unfathomable depths, through a mountain gorge, the sublime entirely overwhelms the sense of sight, and fascinates imagination

The change produced upon the thinking part of man, in passing from the broad St. Lawrence into the seemingly narrow and awfully deep Saguenay, whose waters lave the sides of the towering mountains, which almost shut out the very light of heaven, is such as no pen can paint nor tongue describe.

It is a river one should see if only to know what dreadful aspects nature can assume in her wild moods. Compared to it, the dead sea is blooming, and the wildest ravines look cosy and smiling; it is wild and grand apparently in spite of itself.

On either side rise cliffs varying in perpendicular height from 1,200 to 1,600 feet, and this is the character of the river Saguenay from its mouth to its source.

Ha-Ha-Bay, which is 60 miles from its mouth, affords the first landing and anchorage. The name of this Bay is said to arise from the circumstances of early navigators proceeding in sailing vessels up a river of this kind for 60 miles with eternal sameness of feature, stern and high rocks on which they could not land and no bottom for their anchors, at last broke out into laughing, Ha-Ha, when they found landing and anchorage.

This wonderful river seems one huge mountain rent asunder, there can be little doubt, at some remote age by some great convulsion of nature.

The reader who goes to see it, and all ought to do so who can, for it is one of the great natural wonders of the continent, can add to the poetical filling up of the picture from his own imagination.

This beautiful trip is easy and facile of accomplishment, as new and magnificent boats rivaling in luxuriousness with any in our inland waters, run regularly to Ha-Ha Bay, on board of which the pleasure seeker will experience all that comfort and accommodation which is necessary to the full enjoyment of such a trip.

MONTREAL ADVERTISEMENTS.

RICHMOND SPENCER,
DISPENSING & FAMILY CHEMIST,
Corner of McGill & Notre Dame Streets,
MONTREAL.

IVORY **Hair** Brushes and *Combs* TORTOISE SHELL COMBS, **Tooth** BRUSHES, LOWES, **Brown** and WINDSOR Soap. &c., &c.

LUBIN'S Perfumes, ATKIN- SON'S White Rose AND other EXTRACTS for the Handker- chief. Genuine GERMAN EAU de Cologne

Importer of
DRUGS AND MEDICINES.
Choice English & French **Perfumery,**
TOILET ARTICLES, ELEGANT FANCY GOODS,
&c., &c., &c.
Prescriptions prepared from the purest Chemicals with accuracy.
Homœopathic Medicines always on Hand.
B

RUSSELL HOUSE,

(LATE CLARENDON,)

CORNER OF

Ann & Garden Sts.

Will be run in connection with the

ST. LOUIS HOTEL.

———•———

BUSINESS MEN

Will find arrangements made for their especial accommodation,

At Reasonable Rates for Board,

ALSO :

ELIGIBLE SAMPLE ROOMS

FOR

Commercial Travellers.

Wm. RUSSELL & SON,
PROPRIETORS.

GIBB & Co.

ESTABLISHED 1775.

Merchant Tailors

AND

GENTLEMEN'S HABERDASHERS,

148 St. James Street

MONTREAL.

SIGN OF THE GOLDEN PADLOCK.

L. J. A. SURVEYER,

IMPORTER & DEALER IN

HOUSE FURNISHING

AND

SHELF HARDWARE,

Stoves, Refrigerators,

Baths, Iron Bedsteads

CORNICES, &c., &c.,

524, CRAIG STREET,

MONTREAL.

N. B. Washing Machines, Patent Clothes Wringers, Mangles, Self Heating and Polishing Irons, Sad Iron, Furnaces and Coal Oil.

Stoves always on hand.

The Stadacona Hotel,

LATE RUSSELL'S,

PALACE STREET,

QUEBEC.

This house long and favorably known to the Travelling Public, has been enlarged, newly painted and furnished throughout, and will be ready for the reception of guests on the opening of navigation. It has many advantages, being unrivalled in location, close to the Post Office and principal stores on the leading streets of the City. The subscriber can only say that he will spare no pains to maintain that reputation it has so long held as a First-Class Hotel in this City.

DONALD NOONAN. Proprietor,

Late of Clarendon Hotel.

J. G. PARKS,

Photographer,

FINE STEREOSCOPIC VIEWS

OF

Montreal, Quebec, &c.

FIRST PRIZE 1868 & 1870

AT

Provincial Exhibition.

188 ST. JAMES STREET,

MONTREAL.

VICTOR E. MAUGER,

AGENT FOR THE

WHARFDALE PRINTING PRESSES,

HUGHES & KIMBERS'

Lithographic Gripper Printing Machine

And GUILLOTINE CUTTING MACHINES,

Tangye's Patent Hydraulic Presses.

Depot of Laroche Frères du Martinet, Angonlême, France.

(Fine Writing and Printing Papers.)

Stationers' Sundries, Lithographers' Materials, &c., &c.

VICTOR E. MAUGER, 401 Notre Dame St., Montreal.

(Branch of 110 Reade Street, New York.)

PROWSE BRO'S.,

DEALERS

House Furnishing Hardware,

224 ST. JAMES STREET,

MONTREAL.

Cooking, Parlor, and Hall Stoves, Grates, Iron
Bedsteads, Refrigerators, Baths, Water
Coolers, Planished, Japanned and
Plain Tin Ware,

PLUMBING, GAS FITTING,

COPPERSMITHS.

HOT AIR FURNACES,

TIN AND GALVANIZED IRON ROOFING.

MANUFACTURERS OF

GALVANIZED IRON CORNICES.

B 2

Laurencelle & Vary,

MANUFACTURERS

IMPORTERS OF

French, English & American

BOOTS & SHOES

303 Notre Dame Street

MONTREAL

Visitors and Strangers

TO THE CITY

Are respectfully invited to call at our establishment. We guarantee the quality and finish of our goods and that they will give entire satisfaction.

LAURENCELLE & VARY.

WE HAVE ONLY ONE PRICE

AND THAT IS

MODERATE.

THOMAS & CASTLE

Late of   *Late of*

ANDREW & THOMAS.   **CRAIG & CASTLE.**

HOUSE PAINTERS,

Fresco and General Decorators,

SIGN WRITERS,

PAPERHANGERS, GLAZIERS,

GILDERS, &c.

716 CRAIG STREET

Opposite Alexander St.

Designs & Estimates

GIVEN FOR

PRIVATE DWELLINGS,

CHURCHES,

AND

PUBLIC BUILDINGS.

MAGOG HOUSE,

SHERBROOKE, P.Q.

H. S. HEPBURN,....................Proprietor.

This Hotel has been recently purchased by the present proprietor, and thoroughly repaired and in perfect order. It is now open for the travelling public as a

FIRST CLASS HOUSE,

And being located at a point where the pleasure-seekers to the White Mountains *via* Lake Memphremagog are obliged to spend the night, particular attention will be given to their wants and comfort.

OMNIBUSES AT THE STATION ON ARRIVAL OF EVERY TRAIN.

PAGE'S LINE OF STAGES leave the Hotel every morning, to connect with the steamer *Lady of the Lake*, built expressly for passenger travel, by Captain W. D. Handyside, making two trips daily, and connecting with the Railroad at Newport for the White Mountains, New-York, Boston, and all points South.

ENQUIRE ON ARRIVAL AT THE STATION FOR THE

MAGOG HOUSE.

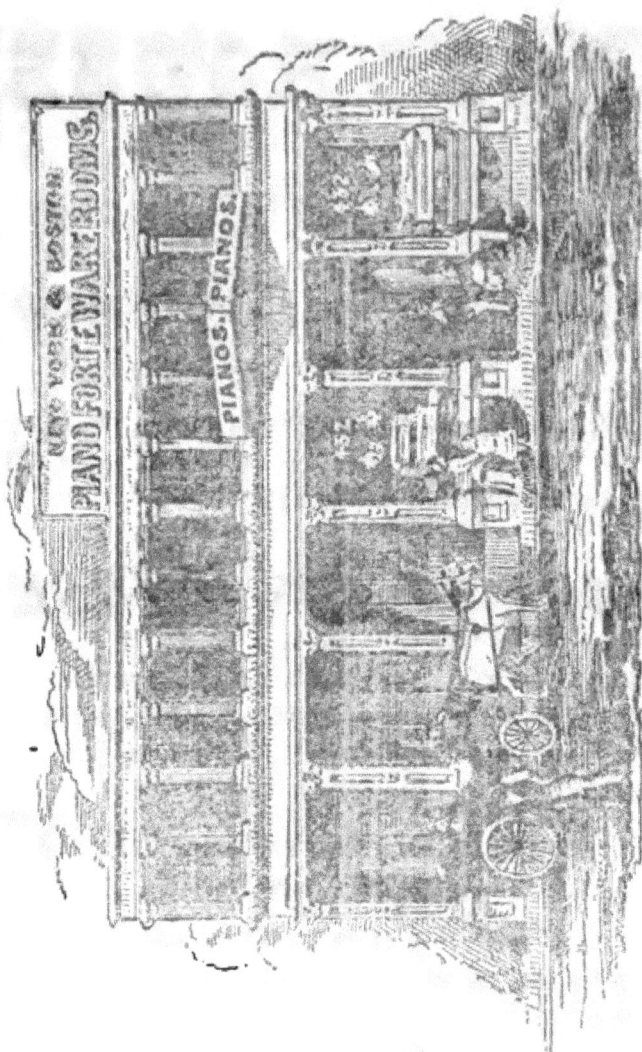

CANADA WIRE WORKS.

THOMAS OVERING,

PRACTICAL WIRE WORKER,

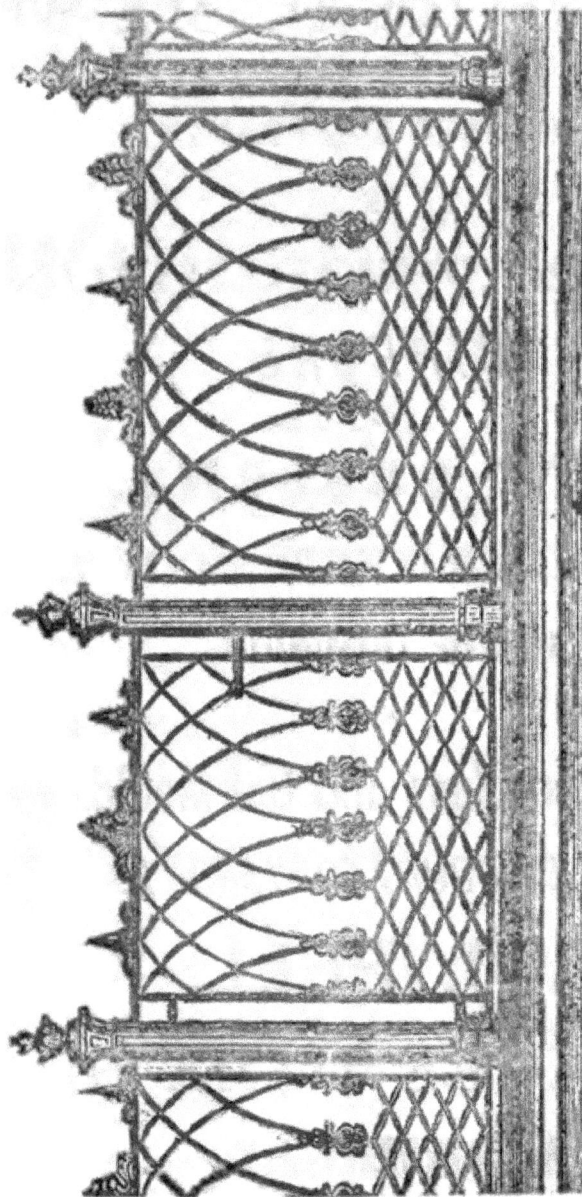

and manufacturer of Fourdrinier and Cylinder Cloths for Paper Mills, Wire-Cloth, Sieves, Riddles, Fenders, Grate and Stove Guards, Meat Safes. Rat and Mouse Traps, Bird Cages, &c.

Particular attention paid to Builders' Work. Cemetery, Garden and Farm Fencing made to order.

757, Craig Street, West of Victoria Square, MONTREAL.

P. O. Box 192½

JOHN MURPHY & Co.
405 Notre Dame St.
CORNER ST. PETER Street.

Bonnett's ⎫
Jaubert's ⎬ Black Silks.
Ponsons ⎭

Pim's ⎫
Arnott's ⎬ Irish Poplins.

Alexandre ⎫
Josephine ⎬ Kid Gloves.

Maltese ⎫
Thread ⎬ Laces.

Maltese ⎫
Thread ⎬ Collars, Sleeves and Handkerchiefs.
Honiton ⎭

Silk ⎫
Thread ⎪
Balbriggan ⎬ Hosiery and Underclothing.
Cotton ⎪
Merino ⎭

Ribbons ⎫
Scarfs ⎪
Sashes ⎬ In great Variety.
Parasols ⎪
Umbrellas ⎭

Irish ⎫
French ⎬ Cambric Handkerchiefs, best makes.

French ⎫
Iron ⎬ Grenadines.
Canvass ⎭

Courtanla's—Black Crapes.

W. R. HIBBARD & CO.

Trunk Factory,

Manufacturers of and dealers in

LADIES' SATCHELS,

Leather Bags,

AND

First-Class Travelling Requisites

356 NotreDame St.

MONTREAL.

Wholesale & **Retail.**

A. BRAHADI,

FIRST PREMIUM

FUR ESTABLISHMENT,

CORNER

Notre Dame & St. Lambert Sts.,

SIGN OF THE LION,

MONTREAL.

N. B.—TOURISTS who may be desirous to purchase CHOICE
FURS, are invited to call and examine the extensive Stock of
LADIES AND GENTLEMEN'S MANUFACTURED FURS.

A. B. was awarded four first-class Medals at the Provincial
Industrial Exhibition at the City of Montreal, in 1860, during the
visit of H. R. H., the Prince of Wales.

DESMARTEAU & BOND,

IMPORTERS OF

Gents Hosiery, Gloves, Ties,

Shirts, Collars, Cuffs, Umbrellas,

SILK AND MERINO

UNDERCLOTHING, &c.

415 NOTRE DAME,

Corner St. Peter Street,

Montreal.

60 OTTAWA HOTEL

McMILLAN & CO.,

Merchant Tailors,

252 ST. JAMES STREET,

Next Door West Ottawa Hotel,

MONTREAL.

Keep Constantly in Stock, everything required in a first Class Tailoring Business.

Gentlemen who wish to enjoy the rare luxury of good fitting pantaloons can be supplied with that article.

Attention given to Ladies Riding Habits.

PRICES MODERATE.

Fixed Prices Strictly Adhered to.

D. NAGY,

FURRIER,

Manufacturer and Importer

ALL KINDS OF

Foreign Furs,

360 NOTRE DAME STREET,

Montreal.

E. BEAUVAIS & CO.,

Dealers in

English, French and American Boots and Shoes.

ALSO

RUBBER GOODS,

293 Notre Dame Street,

OPPOSITE TO H. & H. MERRILL,

MONTREAL.

JAMES MARTIN,

Photographer,

No. 1 BLEURY STREET,

OVER LATHAM'S DRUG STORE

MONTREAL.

PICTURES

TAKEN AT THIS ESTABLISHMENT

IN ANY WEATHER,

AND IN THE

HIGHEST STATE OF PERFECTION

KNOWN IN THE ART.

TERMS MODERATE.

PLEASE GIVE ME A CALL,

And ascertain for yourselves before having Pictures
taken elsewhere.

OTTAWA HOTEL

ALEX GORDON,

PRIZE

PATENT SCALE

MANUFACTURER,

73 COLLEGE STREET,

MONTREAL,

Manufactures and keeps on hand a good assortment of

PATENT

Platform & Counter Scales.

HAY and FORWARDING SCALES
MADE TO ORDER,

Kendall Manufacturing Co'y.

MANUFACTURERS OF THE

"FAVORITE"

KENDALL MANUFAC RING CO.Y, Sewing Machine Manufacturers, and IRON FOUNDERS.

FAVORITE

Office 200, Factory 202, Foundary 198 Craig St,

MONTREAL.

SHUTTLE SEWING MACHINE.

The BEST and CHEAPEST Family Machine in the Market
We are also prepared to execute Orders for LIGHT CASTINGS on reasonable terms.

☞ AGENTS WANTED

In every County not already occupied, to whom the most liberal terms will be offered.

KENDALL MANUFACTURING COMPANY.

C. FITTS & CO.,

Cracker & Biscuit

MANUFACTURERS,

142 INSPECTOR ST.,

BETWEEN

BONAVENTURE & ST. ANTOINE STS.,

MONTREAL.

70   OTTAWA HOTEL

BERNARD BROS.,

Wholesale & Retail

DEALERS IN

Bonnet Silks, Lyons Velvets, Shawls,

JOUVIN'S, ALEXANDRE'S & JOSEPHINE KID GLOVES,

LACES, DRESS GOODS,

Hosiery & Underclothing,

CLOTHS and TWEEDS,

Paragon Frame Umbrellas,

And full lines of Trimmings & Haberdashery.

STRANGERS visiting Montreal will find it greatly to their advantage to call at our establishment before making purchases elsewhere, as we are determined to keep the *Best Assortment of leading Goods* in our line. We will warrant all goods as represented, and one principal feature in our business shall be *Quick Sales and Small Profits.* One Price to all, and GOODS MARKED IN PLAIN FIGURES.

268 Notre Dame St., Montreal.

Opposite Savage, Lyman & Co.'s well known Jewellery Establishment.

BERNARD BROS.

E. BERNARD.   A. BERNARD.   L. BERNARD.

St. Lawrence Metal Stamping Works.

CHARLES STORER,

Metal Stamper & Japanner,

Nos. 204, 206, 208 & 210

CRAIG STREET,

MONTREAL.

Seamless Metal Boxes.

SHEET BRASS, COPPER, ZINC,
IRON, TIN and

BRITTANIA METAL WARES.

Screw Tops for Preserve Jars, Oil Cans, &c.
Metal Checks and Labels.

ADVERTISING SIGNS

on GLASS, METAL, or WOOD, elegant in design,
and First Class Workmanship.

TO TOURISTS.

CENTRAL DRUG STORE,

CORNER

CRAIG & BLEURY STREETS,

MONTREAL.

Constantly in Stock and for sale the following articles:—

Lubin's Perfumes.	Yardley's Toilet Soaps.
Atkinson's do.	Lubin's do.
Rimmel's do.	Condray's do.
Violet's do.	Violet's do.
Genuine Colognes.	Florida Water.
Sponges.	Sponge Bags.
Turkish Towels.	Dressing Cases.

Shell, Horn and Rubber Combs, also, a large assortment of Hair, Nail, Tooth, Cloth, Hat, and Flesh Brushes, and everything usually kept in a **First** Class Drug Store.

COOL SODA WATER FROM THE FOUNTAIN.

Hours of attendance from 7, A.M. to 11, P.M.

R. S. LATHAM, Dispensing Chemist.

Chas. Alexander & Son,

CONFECTIONERS,

"New Cathedral Block,"

CORNER

St. Catherine & University Sts.,

MONTREAL.

The Subscribers have constantly on hand a large assortment of

Cakes, Biscuits, Pastry, &c.,

And choice Sweetmeats fresh daily, also our

NEW REFRESHMENT HALL,

Being now opened, we will have daily all kinds of Ice Cream, Water Ice, &c., Soda Water, Lemonade, Ginger Ale, and Ginger Beer.

STRAWBERRIES & CREAM IN THEIR SEASON

Chas. Alexander & Son,

Corner St. Catherine & University Sts.

"Prince of Wales Hotel,"

LACHINE, QUEBEC.

G. PALLASCIO, Proprietor.

The undersigned having purchased the above Hotel, situated in the

VILLAGE OF LACHINE,

Takes much pleasure in informing the Public, that having refitted and furnished the same for a

First Class Hotel,

He is now prepared to receive and accommodate either transient or permanent boarders, and assures them that no pains will be spared by him to make his Hotel,

A FIRST CLASS RESORT

for pleasure seekers.

The table will at all times be supplied with the delicacies of the season. The Bar with the Choicest of Liquors.

JAMES McCLURE & CO.

393 Notre Dame Street,

MONTREAL.

BRANCH STORE,

ST. CATHERINE STREET,

Immediately West of English Cathedral.

IMPORTERS OF

BRITISH AND AMERICAN

Staple and Fancy Dry Goods,

Hosiery, Gloves & Haberdashery.

SHIRT & COLLAR MANUFACTURERS,

Sole Agents for Mme. Demorest's Patterns.

OTTAWA HOTEL,

LACHINE,

D. O'Brien, - - - - Proprietor.

This house is pleasantly situated, and has been entirely refitted and refurnished, and is one of the most comfortable stopping places in Lachine.

THE BAR,

IS ALWAYS SUPPLIED WITH THE

CHOICEST LIQUORS and CIGARS,

And no pains are spared to minister to the

COMFORT of CALLERS.

Good Stabling & Careful Ostlers.

ST. LAWRENCE

Dye Works,

No. 31 BLEURY STREET,

MONTREAL, P.Q.

JAS. M. McDONALD,

Silk & Woollen Dyer,

SCOURER,

HOT PRESSER, &c.

Gentlemen's Clothes & Feathers Cleaned and Dyed.

KID GLOVES CLEANED.

All ORDERS promptly ATTENDED TO and executed.

OTTAWA HOTEL

Wm. HENRY,

(Late with GIBB & Co.)

236 ST. JAMES ST.,

(2 Doors East of Ottawa Hotel,)

IMPORTER OF

Gentlemen's Haberdashery,

Cartwright & Warner's Merino Goods,
SANGSTER'S UMBRELLAS, &c., &c.

DENT'S TOWN-MADE

KID, DOG, SILK,
AND LISLE GLOVES.

All the latest novelties in

TIES, SCARFS, COLLARS and CUFFS.

SHIRTS & COLLARS
MADE TO ORDER.

BANCROFT & SHARPE'S
City Express and Livery Stables.

Baggage and Parcels CALLED FOR and DELIVERED to any part of the City.

SADDLE HORSES, OPEN & TOP BUGGIES, Family Carriages.

—ALSO—

Large Vehicles for Pleasure Parties
ALWAYS ON HAND.

Office, St. JAMES HOTEL, VICTORIA SQUARE,

Stables, 65 St. Alexander St., opp. St. Patrick's Church.

EVERY MAN
His Own Glass Cutter.

The Carbonized Disc Glass Cutter,

Price only 50 Cts. EACH ONE WARRANTED.

Prepaid by Mail to any part of the Dominion. Supplied at Wholesale on very liberal terms.

AGENTS,

Montreal and East,
CHAS. BROOKS & SON,
LENNOXVILLE, P.Q.

Montreal and West,
JOHN McARTHUR & SON,
MONTREAL, P.Q.

Witherell's Hotel,

PLATTSBURG, N. Y.

———

This First Class Hotel is pleasantly located in the central part of the Village, but a few steps from the

POST OFFICE, TELEGRAPH OFFICE, &c.

The table is furnished with all the delicacies of the season, and every attention paid to the wants and convenience of the Guests.

Tourists, on their way to the

ADIRONDACKS,'

will find no place more pleasant or agreeable than this Hotel.

W. C. LEEKE,
Proprietor.

James Brown & Bro.,

IMPORTERS OF

House Furnishing Hardware.

WASHING MACHINES,
MANGLES,
CLOTHES WRINGERS.

STOVES,

Refrigerators, Registers, &c., &c.

A Call Respectfully Solicited.

No. 219 St. James Street,

MONTREAL.

Robert Houdery,

Working Silversmith,

AND

ELECTRO-PLATER

IN

GOLD, SILVER,

AND NICKEL,

108 St. Peter Street,

MONTREAL.

F. HILL,

Importer of

Piano-Fortes,

Sheet Music,

Parlor Organs,

&c., &c., &c.,

No. 23 VICTORIA SQUARE,

ST. PATRICK'S HALL BUILDING,

MONTREAL.

.